SPEAKING THE WORD
FEARLESSLY

SPEAKING THE WORD FEARLESSLY

Boldness in the New Testament

STANLEY B. MARROW, S.J.

PAULIST PRESS
New York/Ramsey

Copyright © 1982 by
Stanley B. Marrow

Library of Congress
Catalog Card Number: 82-81186

ISBN: 0-8091-2462-9

Published by **Paulist Press**
545 Island Road, Ramsey, N.J. 07446

Printed and bound in the
United States of America

TO J. A. DEVENNY ...

" he bid me goe to the Fountain head,
and read Aristotle, Cicero, Avicenna,
and did call the Neoteriques *****-breeches."

Sanctus resisted them with such constancy that he did not even tell his own name, or the race or the city whence he was, nor whether he was slave or free, but to all questions answered in Latin, "I am a Christian!" This he said for name and city and race and for everything else, and the heathen heard no other sound from him. . . .

His body was a witness to his treatment; it was all one wound and bruise . . . but Christ suffering in him manifested great glory, overthrowing the adversary and showing for the example of the others how there is nothing fearful where there is the love of the Father nor painful where there is the glory of Christ.

(Acts of the Martyrs of Lyons, *around 177 A.D.*)

The modern world is afraid of death. Modern youth is afraid of the modern world. The modern world is afraid of modern youth. The modern world is afraid. . . .

(R. C. Zaehner, Our Savage God, *1974)*

Prefatory Note

Early in 1979 I was invited to deliver an address to the Mile Hi Religious Education Congress in Denver, Colorado. The title chosen by the organizers for my paper on that occasion was "Proclaim His Love Without Fear," which the National Catholic Reporter Cassettes made available for distribution immediately thereafter. It was shortly after I delivered that address that two members of the staff of the Paulist Press approached me with the suggestion of putting it out as a small book. For that gracious suggestion I owe both of them a word of gratitude.

More than a year later, when an opportunity presented itself to fulfill my promise to take that suggestion seriously, I began to realize the difficulty of the seemingly simple task I had resolved to undertake. Transforming a set of brief and sketchy notes into an address to a live and receptive audience was relatively easy compared to ordering the same set of notes into a coherent, publishable whole. Several unsuccessful attempts to set down on paper what I had said in the original address convinced me of the need to commence afresh. Not only the great difference in style between the spoken and the written word but also the quite different nature of the demand for clarity required a different approach.

Thus, it became necessary to start with a more detailed exposition of the two Pauline terms that originally prefaced my remarks: *paraklēsis,* which will be referred to as "the ministry of consolation," and *parrhēsia,* the unhindered liberty of Christian proclamation. Yet, despite the need to recast the whole essay into a new shape, my initial concern remained unaltered. My intention was not simply to expose the meaning of two key terms in Paul's vocabulary of the Christian ministry and mission, but to diagnose the factors that militate against the Christian minister's freedom in the exercise of the ministry of the word in today's world.

Consequently, this little book falls into two parts: one expository, and the other diagnostic. Its aim here is, as it was in the original address, to "exhort, encourage, and console" the ministers of the word in the exercise of their ministry. Should the work succeed in helping even one of them to recover, or perchance to discover, that liberty of speech which is our Christ-won privilege in proclaiming the gospel of life, then it will not have been in vain.

Vigil of Pentecost, 1981

Introduction

*And [Paul] lived there for two whole years . . . and wel-
comed all who came to him, preaching the kingdom of
God and teaching about the Lord Jesus Christ quite openly
and unhindered (Acts 28:30–31).*

When the author of the Book of Acts concluded his
work with these words he was not so much describing an
event as drawing up a program. Christianity was and
remains a missionary movement. Its growth and survival
depend not on genetic proliferation but on the addition to
its members of converts to faith in the Lord Jesus Christ.

*And the Lord added to their number day by day those who
were being saved (Acts 2:47).*

Such a growth in Christianity requires the preaching of
its message to "all nations" (Mt 28:19). This message is,
of course, the gospel, the good news of Jesus Christ,
which calls to conversion to a new life, a turning away
from idols "to serve a living and true God" (1 Thes 1:9).
But because such conversion is not merely a matter of
intellectual assent but of a whole life lived in the newness
of the Spirit, the preaching of the gospel has to be
addressed to believers as well as to non-believers, to those
of the household of faith as well as to those who "sit in

darkness and in the shadow of death" (Lk 1:79). This is the primary task of the Church and of its ministers. The Church's ministry is therefore first and foremost a ministry of the word. Everything else is subordinated to this, even the sacraments:

> For Christ did not send me to baptize but to preach the gospel (1 Cor 1:17).

So it is all the more regrettable that in a time of spiritual crisis and doctrinal confusion this basic fact of Christianity is, if not altogether overlooked, at least given inadequate attention. In the current debate on ministry and ordination—to take but one example—the primacy of the word is relegated to the background as a presumed premise and is hardly examined with the care and attention it requires. Indeed we seem scarcely to notice that many individuals in the Church today carry on a ministry of the word without "ordination."

> And how can men preach unless they are sent? (Rom 10:15).

This is a question that needs extensive reflection because it involves far more than the act of mounting a pulpit and carrying out a liturgical function. The ministry of the word in the Church embraces all those tasks of teaching, instructing, catechizing, exhorting, admonishing, comforting, encouraging, and consoling, as well as preaching, in the common acceptance of the term. For every time a Christian brings the gospel message to bear on the life of another, that Christian is exercising the ministry of the word. The Sunday school teacher, the missionary in distant lands, the priest in the pulpit, the theologian in the classroom, and the Pope on the balcony of Saint Peter's—all exercise the ministry of the word in the Church. Each brings to those who would listen the good news of salvation in Christ Jesus.

It is for those engaged in such a ministry, whether they are officially "ordained" or not, that the following pages are principally addressed. It is especially for those who have dedicated their lives to instructing Christians of all ages in the meaning of the gospel message that these pages are written. Whatever term one might choose to describe it in a diocesan directory, a school catalogue, or a parochial bulletin, the ministry of such Christians is a ministry of the word. It is, alas, a ministry made more difficult today by the confusion of views about its nature and by the disparity of opinions about its exercise.

The scope of this little book, however, is limited to a description of the nature of this ministry of the word as a ministry of consolation, and to an analysis of the freedom that must characterize its exercise. The endeavor might best be described as a reflection on two New Testament terms: *paraklēsis* (the ministry of consolation) and *parrhēsia* (the unhindered liberty of proclamation). It is certainly arguable that the ministry of the word in the Church is precisely one of consolation only insofar as such a word is proclaimed without hindrance, in total freedom and with what has been defined as the "unhindered frankness of privilege." In other words, the proclamation of the gospel message and the exhortation to Christian life are the exercise of that sovereign freedom for which "Christ has set us free" (Gal 5:1).

Lest these introductory remarks give rise to false expectations about the scope of this reflection, it should be said at the outset that its principal concern is not with the grave problem of the relation between the ecclesiastical teaching authorities and the professional theologians in the Church. It would be pretentious even to attempt a contribution to the current discussion of this far from easy problem within the severely restricted limits of this work. What is said here is, of course, applicable to the participants in that discussion no less than it is to the humblest catechist in some obscure corner of the globe. The liberty to proclaim the word without fear is a gift that belongs to the lowliest preacher or catechism teacher no less than it does to the great names in theology and the recognized authorities in the Church. Indeed, it is my conviction that the threat to the liberty of the lowly ministers of the word today is far more serious and more damaging than all the threats to "professional theologians" which, whether real or imagined, capture the headlines in today's media.

The Ministry of Consolation

Of all the words employed by the New Testament to describe the Christian ministry of the word (gospel, kerygma, instruction, exhortation, etc.) the word *paraklēsis*, from which we have the English "paraclete," is the most comprehensive in its implications. It combines the meanings denoted by the other available terms and conveys nuances common to many of them. The better to make this observation clear, let us look at the Greek term and its uses.

Paraklēsis is a noun derived from the verb which means: "to call for," "to summon," "to invite," "to beseech," "to ask for help." Though the verb is frequent

6

throughout the New Testament, the writings of Saint Paul alone account for more than half the instances of its occurrence. This is even truer of the noun *paraklēsis*. Its various meanings have to be kept in mind, of course; but its most common and frequent meaning in Paul—as also in the Book of Acts—is "exhortation by the Word proclaimed in the power of the Holy Ghost" (Schmitz, p. 794).

When Paul writes to the Thessalonians, "I beseech and exhort you" (1 Thes 4:1), or to the Corinthians, "I appeal to you" (1 Cor 1:10; Rom 15:30; 12:1), or when he describes the charism of apostolic preaching as "exhortation" (Rom 12:6-8), he is using the same Greek word to describe that "ministry of reconciliation" (2 Cor 5:18) which is always an address, an appeal, an admonition and an exhortation. But—and this is important to keep in mind always—it is all these "in Christ" (Phil 2:1), "in the Lord Jesus" (1 Thes 4:1), "by the name of our Lord Jesus Christ" (1 Cor 1:10), "by our Lord Jesus Christ and the love of the Spirit" (Rom 15:30), "by the meekness and gentleness of Christ" (2 Cor 10:10), "by the mercy of God" (Rom 12:1). Clearly then such a ministry is entirely within the context of Christian salvation. It proclaims this salvation, reminds the hearers of it, recalls its implications for their individual lives, and sets them on guard against counterfeit substitutes. For in order that the ministry of the word be truly a ministry of reconciliation, it must always be within the context of the proclamation of that event which, in Christ Jesus, sets us free from the shackles of law, of sin, and of death. It is always within the context of the proclamation of salvation.

Now, whenever this saving event is proclaimed, it is always proclaimed as a call to a new life. It is not, and must never become, merely the elaboration of some philosophic system, even if the system be hallowed by centuries of usage; nor is it merely the detailing of ethical demands or moral imperatives, however necessary and urgent these may be. The proclamation is always a challenge to a newness of life. Such a new life can only follow upon the death of the old self, the abandonment of all past securities, the relinquishing of any imagined claims on salvation. The proclamation of salvation is the proclamation of a grace: a gift that is neither earned nor earnable. It calls for a turning away from all our past idols whence we sought our redemption and deliverance in order that we might wholeheartedly and exclusively "serve a living and true God" (1 Thes 1:9).

The proclamation of salvation is a call to accept unequivocally that God, and God alone, is "the source of your life in Christ Jesus" (1 Cor 1:30); that in this same Christ Jesus "all things are yours . . . whether the world or life or death or the present or the future, all are yours" (1 Cor 3:22). To live out this response in our day to day lives, to resist all the allures and enticements of other means of salvation—whatever credentials they offer and however facile they seem to be, to refuse to accept any other gospel, even if preached by "an angel from heaven" (Gal 1:8), to shoulder fully the awesome burden of that freedom for which "Christ has set us free" (Gal 5:1), is something that requires the constant entreaty, exhortation, supplication, and consolation of the ministry of the word, which Paul describes as *paraklēsis*. This is ultimately why there must always be preachers, teachers, catechists and instructors in the Church everywhere. Their task is never ended no matter how thriving and vibrant the community they address is. They have to call constantly to a life, a life "in Christ Jesus." They have to remind their hearers over and over again to "have this mind among yourselves, which is yours in Christ Jesus" (Phil 2:5). They never cease to call the believers to a conduct "worthy of the gospel of Jesus Christ" (Phil 1:27), nor are they ever finished bringing that same gospel to non-believers.

Every minister of the word, whatever the current designation of his or her particular task, proclaims the fact of salvation in Jesus Christ. Because the response to this message is a whole life lived in Christ and for others, and because such a life is a constant demand to die to self in order to live in him, because it is a life that necessarily and unavoidably involves suffering and is constantly subject to that subtlest and most insidious of temptations, the temptation to grow "weary in well-doing" (Gal 6:9; 2 Thes 3:13), the ministry of the word must always be a ministry of encouragement and exhortation, of comfort and consolation. This is no easy task. Unlike so many other human and social services, for which it is all too frequently mistaken and with which it is often confused, it requires nothing less than the total gift of self on the part of the proclaimer, a readiness to share "not only the gospel of God but also our own selves" (1 Thes 2:8).

The minister of the word must, moreover, ever keep in mind that

We are ambassadors for Christ, God making his appeal through us (2 Cor 5:20).

As ministers of the word, we do not stand on our own. Our ultimate reliance is not on our power, whether it be our power of speech or of wisdom or of learning. The

9

authority behind our appeal, the supreme authority behind our proclamation, is that the word we speak is not our own but God's. It is a constant miracle that it is accepted

> *not as the word of men but as what it really is, the word of God (1 Thes 2:13).*

We work "together with him" (2 Cor 6:1) in order that the faith of our hearers

> *might not rest in the wisdom of men but in the power of God (1 Cor 2:5).*

Our confidence to proclaim that word and our assurance and freedom in speaking it do not derive from ourselves, whether from our academic accomplishments, our natural endowments, or our acquired skills, but solely from God who alone

> *gives life to the dead and calls into existence the things that do not exist (Rom 4:17).*

In today's world, which in so many ways is not unlike Corinth and Thessalonica in the first century, where the properly packaged word is a source of power and a means of livelihood, the Christian minister of the word must remember that

> *We are not, like so many, peddlers of God's word; but as men of sincerity, as commissioned by God, in the sight of God we speak in Christ (2 Cor 2:17).*

The constant temptation that faces us is to emulate the

successful "peddlers" of the word, captivated as we can be by the inescapable evidence of statistical graphs and economic histograms. The status of such "peddlers" of the word in our society, their winning ways, the vast audiences they command, and the envy and adulation they arouse continue to exert their subtle influence on ministers of the word in every rank and of every description. Everything is fair game toward gaining a "good press." And yet:

> *Our appeal does not spring from error or uncleanness, nor is it made with guile; but just as we have been approved by God to be entrusted with the gospel, so we speak, not to please men, but to please God who tests our hearts. For we never used either words of flattery, as you know, or a cloak for greed, as God is witness; nor did we seek glory from men, whether from you or from others, though we might have made demands as apostles of Christ (1 Thes 2:3-6).*

Indeed, the very opposite of this attitude is what marks the true Christian minister of the word, as Paul goes on to say in this same passage to the Thessalonians:

> *But we were gentle among you, like a nurse taking care of her children. So, being affectionately desirous of you, we were ready to share with you not only the gospel of God but also our own selves, because you had become very dear to us. For you remember our labor and toil, brethren; we worked night and day, that we might not burden any of you, while we preached to you the gospel of God (1 Thes 2:7-9)*

Our *paraklēsis* (appeal) is not made with the "error" of misconceptions, nor with the "uncleanness" of hidden agenda, nor with the "guile" of hucksters. But our appeal is as ministers "entrusted with the gospel" who couple their deep affection for their hearers with a readiness to share their very selves with them. This is why the ministry of word can never be a sinecure. It requires labor and toil and work night and day.

Of course, no one is going to deny that "the laborer deserves his wages" (Lk 10:7; 1 Cor 9:4; 1 Tim 5:18). But this is a far cry from the attitude that regards the ministry as just another means of gaining a livelihood, just another "profession" among so many others. It takes a great deal more than "labor and toil . . . night and day." It requires nothing short of giving "our own selves" to those to whom we minister. Only then can we say without posturing:

> *You are witnesses, and God also, how holy and righteous and blameless was our behavior to you believers; for you know how, like a father with his children, we exhorted each one of you and encouraged you and charged you to lead a life worthy of God, who calls you into his own kingdom and glory (1 Thes 2:10-12).*

In this whole second chapter of 1 Thessalonians, Paul draws up a list of what makes the ministry a *paraklēsis*. The ministry does not spring from error, or uncleanness, or guile; it is not motivated by flattery, or greed, or the quest for the glory of men. The ministers of the word have a deep sense of the divine approval, a sense of mission. It is because of this that they reveal, not the hectoring tyranny of a demagogue, but a tender gentleness like that of a mother nursing her infant. Their whole ministry reveals their affectionate desire and readiness to share, not just the gospel, but their own selves as well. It

12

is this that makes the ministry a "labor night and day," a work that is holy, righteous and blameless. This is what makes the exhortation, the encouragement, and the charge (or "witness," as the Greek has it) of the minister so much "like a father with his children." Such a task involved for Saint Paul, as it involves for anyone who seriously undertakes it, suffering, shameful treatment, and great opposition. And this is precisely where the need for genuine courage comes in.

Though we had already suffered and been shamefully treated . . . we had courage in our God to declare to you the gospel of God in the face of great opposition (1 Thes 2:2).

The minister of the word must, moreover, keep ever in mind that this word is a word of salvation in Christ Jesus, a "gospel," not a panacea for all human ills, or a program for international development, or an antidote to the misery of mankind. Of course, it could be and could very well do many of these things; but a little knowledge of history must temper our optimism and give some measure to our expectations and claims.

What the word proclaims to the world is that Jesus Christ, through his death on the cross and his resurrection, has set us free from sin (Rom 6:18), from the law (Rom 7:4), and from death (1 Cor 15:54-55).

The sting of death is sin, and the power of sin is the law. But thanks be to God, who gives us the victory through our Lord Jesus Christ (1 Cor 15:56).

The word has to remind believers as well as declare to unbelievers that we are *discharged from the law, dead to that which held us captive, so that we serve not under the old written code but in the new life of the Spirit (Rom 7:6).*

It can never tire of repeating to a world that forever clings to the reassuring comfort of the law, that is ever ready to embrace the temporary triumphs over death, and that prefers the comforts of piety to the exigencies of life for others:

There is therefore now no condemnation for those who are in Christ Jesus. For the law of the Spirit of life in Christ Jesus has set me free from the law of sin and death (Rom 8:1-2).

This is the meaning of the salvation we proclaim: the gift of sovereign freedom, not only from sin and from the law, but from death itself. Death, the ultimate alienation from all we know and everyone we love, is at the root of all our sins. The serpent of the creation narrative is always there to reassure us, "You will not die" (Gen 3:4). But the good news in Christ, who died with "a loud cry" (Mk 15:37), knows better than that. It proclaims to all those who "sit in darkness and in the shadow of death" not the abolition of death, but Christ's victory over it. The ministry of the word is genuinely a ministry of consolation because it is a constant reminder—and a much needed one—that in Christ Jesus death itself lost its sting:

Death is swallowed up in victory.
O death, where is thy victory?
O death, where is thy sting? (1 Cor 15:54-55).

One would have thought that such freedom is inalienable, that once a Christian knows its intoxication there can be no turning back, no hankering after the slavery of the past. But this gift of freedom is a gift of faith that requires the toppling of all our idols, the overturning of all our values, the abandonment of all our former sources of confidence and security:

He who finds his life will lose it and he who loses his life for my sake will find it (Mt 10:39).

But relinquishing "one's life" is never easy; the very prospect of it induces panic and makes us grasp for the old, proven, tangible security of what Paul calls "the glory of men." Faith is a venture. It is not a once for all decision but a lifelong series of decisions, each requiring a death to self:

For while we live we are always being given up to death for Jesus' sake, so that the life of Jesus may be manifested in our mortal flesh (2 Cor 4:11);

As it is written, "For thy sake we are being killed all the day long; we are regarded as sheep to be slaughtered" (Rom 8:36; see Psalm 44:22).

The "always being given up to death" and the "all day long" should convince us that both passages speak of more than the heroic act of martyrdom for the faith. They speak of the constant risk in any Christian's life and, consequently, of the ubiquitous temptation to grasp at all the facile and ready assurances of security and salvation that the word and its religions offer us as escapes from the need to die to self.

This is why Christians always stand in need of those who bring them the true word of salvation, encourage their faltering steps, console their sagging spirits, and comfort their failing strength. They need ministers who remind them over and over again that salvation is and remains an unearned gift; that he who died for us "while we were yet helpless," "while we were yet sinners," "while we were enemies" (Rom 5:6, 8, 10) will not abandon us or withdraw his gift; that our only and true salvation comes from his death for us on the cross. Christians have always needed, as they need especially today, the consolation of knowing that

we walk by faith, not by sight (2 Cor 5:7),

and that all those who try to supplant or supplement this faith by logical proofs, historical demonstration, extraordinary manifestations, or the evanescent thrills of pious practices or religious "experiences" are impotent charlatans among so many that crowd the thoroughfares of modern life, offering salvation at a discount and jostling for numerical advantage in a statistical wilderness. It is the task of the ministers of the word to remind Christians constantly of the freedom that is theirs and to safeguard it against all the ersatz forms of deliverance and the bogus claims of instant salvation proffered by individuals or by institutions, howsoever holy they seem and no matter how demonstrably successful they might happen to be.

The ministry of the word is a *paraklēsis* because it embraces the whole of a Christian's life in all its varied aspects. It is a ministry of "consolation" because, as an author recently explained, "to console" is more than merely to scatter abroad a few items of good news. It is rather to communicate the good news. It helps us to discover the meaning of our lives, but also of our deaths; of our encounters with others, but also of our loneliness; of our toil and striving, but also of our failure; of our loves, but also of the violence and the hatred that seethe within us. This ministry helps us not only to situate ourselves vis-à-vis the truth, but to do the truth (cf. Jn 3:21). It does not teach a doctrine, but enlightens a whole life and invites all hearers to return to the path of truth. It does not propose a coherence on the abstract level of explanations, but allows each one to realize the coherence of his own existence. Finally, "to console" is to allow each one of us to discover his own freedom, not only when we succeed in subjecting the course of events to our own will and desire, but also when we feel crushed by the weight of circumstances, when we feel victimized by an inevitable, inexorable and blind destiny (Thomas, p. 69).

This then is the reason why the ministry of the word is a word of comfort, of consolation, a *paraklēsis*. This Greek vocable has aptly been described as "the wooing proclamation of salvation" (Schmitz, p. 795). The Greek word did not originally manifest the prevalence of this meaning of "consolation" in its usage. It was when the Hebrew Old Testament came to be translated into Greek that this meaning emerged. The New Testament thus had ready to hand a word already charged with the meaning of God's mercy and salvation. It is not without reason that Second Isaiah (Is 40-55) is called "The Book of the Consolation of Israel":

Comfort, comfort my people, says your God.
Speak tenderly to Jersualem,

17

and cry to her that her warfare is ended,
that her iniquity is pardoned . . . (Is 40:1-2).

I, I am he that comforts you;
who are you that you are afraid of man who dies,
of the son of man who is made like grass . . ." (Is 51:12).

It is this same God who has revealed to us "the light of the gospel of the glory of Christ," "who has shone in our hearts to give the light of the knowledge of the glory of God in the face of Christ" (2 Cor 4:4, 6). This is why Paul calls God "the God of encouragement (*paraklēsis*)" (Rom 15:5) and why he speaks of the "encouragement (*paraklēsis*) of the scriptures" (Rom 15:4).

The ministry of the word is therefore a ministry of encouragement, of comfort, and of consolation. But these are not the heartwarming effects of camaraderie and comradeship, but the gift of salvation.

For what we preach is not ourselves, but Jesus Christ as Lord, with ourselves as your servants for Jesus' sake (2 Cor 4:5).

What lies behind these terms of "encouragement," "comfort," and "consolation" is not the personal magnetism and charm, the intellectual achievements and the learning, or even the piety and charism of the minister, but only and solely the power of God who, in Christ Jesus, has set us free from sin, from the law, and from death. *Paraklēsis* is a ministry of consolation because it is an integral part of the mystery of salvation.

But how are men to call upon him in whom they have not believed? And how are they to believe in him of whom they

18

have never heard? And how are they to hear without a preacher? (Rom 10:14).

The Freedom To Proclaim

To proclaim the freedom won for us by Christ is a perilous undertaking. Its deadliest danger is not, as is often alleged, the libertinism which confuses liberty with license, and to which such proclamation can and sometimes does lead. Its deadliest enemy by far is our own fear of freedom itself. Deny it as we might, freedom frightens us not only by the inescapable responsibility it puts squarely on our shoulders, but by stripping us of the specious security to which our slavery has accustomed us. The Roman philosopher Seneca summed it up well when he said, "Slavery holds a few in its grip, but many more hold fast to slavery" (Epistle XXII). Yet it is precisely our freedom from slavery, our liberty in Christ, that is at the very heart of the message we proclaim, the call to newness of life.

But the gift of liberty in Christ is given us not for ourselves only but for others. It sets us free in our dealing with God by giving us the ready access of children to the Father. It sets us free in our dealings with others by giving us the grace to turn to them in order "to serve and not to be served" (cf. Mk 10:45). To those who serve others in the ministry of the word, this liberty is manifested in the characteristically Christian "freedom of speech" in proclaiming the gospel of salvation, "not from error, or from uncleanness, or with guile," "without flattery, greed, and the search for the glory of men" (cf. 1 Thes 2).

This "freedom of speech" in the proclamation of the

19

gospel, in the exercise of *paraklēsis*, is expressed in the New Testament by the typically Greek term of *parrhēsia*. It is typically Greek because, unlike so many other New Testament terms (e.g., "Church," "covenant," "holy," etc.), it does not come to the New Testament from the Septuagint, the Greek translation of the Hebrew Old Testament, where its occurrence is extremely limited. So, in order to understand the extent of its meaning in the New Testament, we have to look at the use of *parrhēsia* in the Greek world.

Parrhēsia is a word that belongs to the political vocabulary of the Greek city state. Literally, it means "to say everything." In the context of democracy in a city state it expresses the "right of the free citizen to express his opinion in the assembly" (van Unnik, p. 471). It is interesting to note that the name of that assembly in Greek is *ekklēsia*, the term used for the assembly of the people of God in the Septuagint, and for the Church in the New Testament.

As the essential mark of Greek democracy (Schlier, p. 871), *parrhēsia* is the most esteemed possession of its citizens. There is no loss greater than its loss (Schlier, p. 872). As Pericles, the real founder of Athenian democracy, reminded the citizens of Athens in his funeral oration on those who had died in the Peloponnesian War, "We do not say that a man who takes no interest in politics is a man who minds his own business; we say that he has no business here at all. We Athenians, in our own persons, take our decisions on policy or submit them to proper discussion: for we do not think that there is an incompatibility between words and deeds . . ." (Thucydides, *The Peloponnesian War,* Book Two, chapter 4).

The right of the free citizen to say anything publicly

carried with it, as any right does, the corresponding obligation to be open to the truth. Such openness to the truth, an openness that resists both the tendency of things to hide themselves from us and our own tendency to avert our gaze from reality—for "Human kind/Cannot bear very much reality"—is another meaning of *parrhēsia* in the public sphere. Such openness to the truth requires great courage. It is what is meant by "candor": an unblinking gaze at the whole truth and an unhindered freedom in its expression. By safeguarding the right of the citizens to say anything in the assembly, *parrhēsia* keeps "the reality of things open in candid objectivity" (Schlier, p. 873).

In the private sphere *parrhēsia* denotes "that free intercourse between friends who speak the truth and do not flatter one another" (van Unnik, p. 471). It marks the ease of exchange between friends who are sure enough of their love for one another to speak the plain truth without foisting on the other a false image of oneself, which would be insincerity, or a falsified estimate of the other, which would be flattery. In other words, *parrhēsia* speaks freely while, in so doing, it is careful to keep the freedom of the other intact. Socrates, as Laches describes him in Plato's Dialogue that bears his name, was a good example of someone whose words were "noble sentiments and complete freedom of speech (*parrhēsia*)" (Plato, *Laches* 188 E).

Of course, like all good things, such "freedom of speech" can be abused. It then becomes "impudence" or "insolence" or "shamelessness" (Schlier, p. 874). So *parrhēsia* came to mean such abuse of the privilege. It came to be applied to certain philosophers of the day who, because they esteemed *parrhēsia* as one of the highest ideals, "with great insolence hurled their invectives against everybody" (van Unnik, p. 471). The limit to the exercise of freedom is always defined by the freedom of others. Trespass such a limit, and the privilege is abused.

The fortunes of *parrhēsia* need surprise no one acquainted with the evolution of language and the indignities to which words are subjected in daily use. But it is necessary to keep in mind not only the genesis of such words but also their original meaning which often enough manages to cling to them through their varied histories. The notion of liberty in Greece did not always include the freedom of speech. In the archaic period greater value was set upon "silence and reticence" (Momigliano, p. 184) as virtues that should grace the good man. It was Athenian democracy of the fifth century B.C. that stressed the right of citizens to say everything (*parrhēsia*). Later, as democratic institutions declined, *parrhēsia* became "more of a private virtue (the courage to speak frankly) than a political right" (Momigliano, p. 185). But even as a "refined art of social relation" it eventually came to mean flattery of the feared and insolence toward the despised. Whether the ebbing fortunes of the term describe a general tendency of language in general or the more lamentable human tendency to abuse our prized and precious gifts might make an interesting topic for discussion; but the fortunes of *parrhēsia* will always serve as a salutary parable in either case.

The Term in the Septuagint

The relatively infrequent use of *parrhēsia* in the Septuagint contributes two important elements to our understanding of the term in the New Testament.

1. In the Greek Old Testament *parrhēsia* is a gift of God that marks the free man from the slave. Leviticus 26:13 in the Hebrew Old Testament reads:

I am the Lord your God, who brought you forth out of the land of Egypt, that you should not be their slaves; and I have broken the bars of your yoke and made you walk erect.

But in the Greek translation this last phrase reads:

and brought you forth with parrhēsia.

So this *parrhēsia* (boldness) is seen as a gift of God to his people. It is, moreover, God's own Wisdom that possesses *parrhēsia*:

Wisdom cries aloud in the street;
in the market she raises her voice (Prov 1:20),

which the Septuagint renders, "in the broad places she *speaks boldly.*"

2. Such a gift of God to his people finds expression in their "open access to Him with no more let or hindrance" (Schlier, p. 876):

And if you turn and humble yourself before the Lord . . .
you shall have boldness *before the Lord . . . (Job 22:23,26*
in the Septuagint).

It is this confidence, this "boldness before the Lord," that marks the prayer of the just. *Parrhēsia* is thus "the freedom of the righteous towards God expressed in prayer" (Schlier, p. 876).

The new elements contributed to the meaning of *parrhēsia* by the Septuagint are therefore the view that it is a gift of God, associated with the divine Wisdom, and manifested in the just man's ready and unhindered access to God which finds expression particularly in prayer. Except for such Jewish writers of the first century as Philo of Alexandria and the historian Josephus, *parrhēsia* in Greek literature was a word that belonged to the political and the private spheres, but not to the religious. So, despite its restricted usage in the Old Testament, and despite its typically Greek use in the New, the elements contributed to its meaning by the Septuagint do find echoes in its use by at least one part of the New Testament: the Johannine writings.

The Johannine Writings

It is with the Johannine writings that our examination of *parrhēsia* in the New Testament must start. The reason is not only the bridge that these writings provide between the use of the term in the Septuagint and in the New Testament, but also the fact that John is the only one of the four evangelists to use the term. The term does occur once in the first three: in Mark's description of Jesus' first prediction of the passion:

And he began to teach them that the Son of man must suffer many things. ... And he said this plainly *(Mk 8:31–32).* *

---

* Because the RSV uses a variety of words to translate *parrhēsia*, the word so translated will henceforth be italicized in the Scriptural citations.

24

But it is in John's Gospel, where Jesus is the incarnate Wisdom, that we encounter the use of *parrhēsia* to describe the person of Jesus and his work:

I have spoken openly *to the world. ... I said nothing secretly (Jn 18:20).*

There was no mistaking the meaning of what Jesus had said:

Ask those who have heard me, what I said to them; they know what I said (Jn 18:21).

This was Jesus' response to the high priest who questioned him "about his disciples and his teaching" (Jn 18:19). The people of Jerusalem knew this too:

Is not this the man whom they seek to kill? And here he is, speaking openly *(Jn 7:25-26).*

His own brothers had urged him to leave Galilee and go to Judea:

For no man works in secret if he seeks to be known openly *(Jn 7:4).*

According to John, Jesus took their advice and "went up, not *publicly,* but in private" (Jn 7:10). The rest of John 7 is an admirable illustration of Jesus' sovereign freedom to speak openly in the face of opposition and of danger to life itself (Jn 7:20,25,27,30,32). Those who heard him had to admit:

No man ever spoke like this man! (Jn 7:46).

25

What Jesus revealed to them was not only the nature of his mission (Jn 7:37; 8:12,28–29) but also the precious gift that he brought them:

So if the Son makes you free, you will be free indeed (Jn 8:36).

But it takes boldness to accept this gift, and even more boldness to exercise it:

Yet for fear of the Jews no one spoke openly *of him (Jn 7:13).*

Nowhere does the sharp contrast between *parrhēsia* and its opposite, "fear," receive sharper definition.

The Fourth Gospel employs *parrhēsia* to describe the work of the Revealer who prepares his disciples for the day "when I shall no longer speak to you in figures but tell you *plainly* of the Father" (Jn 16:25). This promise is immediately followed by the assurance of their ready access to the Father in prayer:

In that day you will ask in my name; and I do not say to you that I shall pray the Father for you; for the Father himself loves you (Jn 16:26–27).

And the disciples of Jesus are not slow to understand him:

Ah, now you are speaking plainly, *not in any figure! (Jn 16:29).*

Such "plain speaking" about the Father by the Revealer opens up a ready and unhindered access for the believers in their approach to the Father in their prayers. The theme of this ready access finds even fuller elaboration in the First Letter of John, where the gift of *parrhēsia*, "of confidence before God," is described in function of our faith in the Revealer and of our concomitant obedience to his commandment. It is obedience to this commandment that "casts out fear" (1 Jn 4:18):

> *If our hearts do not condemn us, we have* confidence *before God; and we receive from him whatever we ask, because we keep his commandments and do what pleases him (1 Jn 3:21–22).*

> *And this is the* confidence *which we have in him, that if we ask anything according to his will he hears us (1 Jn 5:14).*

Parrhēsia in 1 John—as also in the Letter to the Hebrews, but in a slightly different context—describes a distinctive mode of being that is appropriate to the Christian. It describes the boldness of our access to God as Father as well as our fearless confidence in him as Judge. Of course, a great deal more could—and perhaps should—be said about how willing Christians are to barter away this liberty in exchange for the evanescent comforts and consolations promised by the "spiritual" techniques and gimmicks purveyed by the various gurus of this or that "spirituality." But the scope of this brief work is limited, by a prior option, to *parrhēsia* as it characterizes the public proclamation of the gospel message.

The Acts of the Apostles

For *parrhēsia* as a characteristic of the Christian proc-

27

lamation of the gospel we must turn to the Acts of the Apostles and to the letters of Saint Paul. Of course, we have to keep in mind the obvious and close link that binds readiness of access to God in prayer with the fearless proclamation of the gospel. There is in the New Testament no strictly "secular" use of the term *parrhēsia.* Its use in the Johannine writings and in the Letter to the Hebrews is more readily understood by the link to its use in the Septuagint, while its use in Acts and in Paul is better understood by its various meanings in the political and personal spheres of the Greek world. Nevertheless, both in one and the other group of writings, the term receives its true meaning from the context of salvation in Christ Jesus.

We find the widest use of *parrhēsia* in the New Testament in the Book of Acts and in the writings of Saint Paul. In these writings we see the typically Greek meaning of the term put to admirable use when applied to the proclamation of the Christian message. Indeed, the term is so closely allied to the proclamation of the message that it becomes almost synonymous with preaching itself: preaching *"boldly* in the name of Jesus" (Acts 9:27), *"boldly* in the name of the Lord" (9:28), speaking *"boldly* of the Lord" (14:3), etc. In the Book of Acts it is the Lord himself who gives the ministers of his word the *parrhēsia* to speak publicly with courage and candor:

And now, Lord . . . grant to thy servants to speak thy word with all boldness *(Acts 4:29).*

. . . they were filled with the Holy Spirit and spoke the word of God with boldness *(Acts 4:31).*

To speak the word of the Lord boldly and openly to a

hostile and indifferent world is the work of the Holy Spirit, a charism. As at the beginning of the Church there is a Pentecost, so throughout the Church's history, that same Spirit enables its ministers to preach the kingdom of God and to teach about the Lord Jesus Christ "quite openly and unhindered" (Acts 28:31). The ministers of the word, the proclaimers of the good news, need never question the freedom that is theirs to speak openly, candidly, and forcefully to a hostile world or to a deaf Church. If they have amply justified misgivings about themselves and their individual talents, they need never question the gift itself that is theirs in the Spirit of the Lord. Their *parrhēsia* is an unearned gift, not an attainment; and therein lies its irresistible force.

In the Book of Acts it is particularly Paul's missionary activity that is most characterized by this sovereign freedom to proclaim boldly and fearlessly the message of salvation to all. Barnabas describes to the Jerusalem disciples how Paul at Damascus "had preached *boldly* in the name of Jesus" (Acts 9:27); and Paul himself

> *went in and out among them at Jerusalem preaching* boldly *in the name of the Lord (Acts 9:28).*

That was what marked his preaching at Antioch of Pisidia (Acts 13:46), at Iconium (Acts 14:3), at Ephesus (Acts 19:8), and before King Agrippa (Acts 26:26). Paul's freedom of speech in Acts is not simply a freedom of speech in the face of great danger, but, as often as not, his very freedom of speech created dangers (Acts 9:23; 13:45; 14:5; 19:9).

In this regard the picture of Paul in Acts reflects faithfully the image we have of him from his own letters.

29

In his First Letter to the Thessalonians, the earliest document in our New Testament, Paul describes his work:

Though we had already suffered and been shamefully treated at Philippi, as you know, we had courage *in our God to declare to you the gospel of God in the face of great opposition (1 Thes 2:2).*

The Letter to the Ephesians, which though perhaps not Paul's own is nevertheless a compendium of his writings, asks the readers to

make supplication . . . also for me that utterance may be given me in opening my mouth boldly *to proclaim the mystery of the gospel, for which I am an ambassador in chains; that I may declare it* boldly, *as I ought to speak (Eph 6:19–20).*

The reference to Paul's imprisonment must be kept in mind when we read Philippians, a letter which he wrote while in prison and awaiting trial (Phil 1:12–26):

Yes, and I shall rejoice. For I know that through your prayers and the help of the Spirit of Jesus Christ this will turn out for my deliverance, as it is my eager expectation and hope that I shall not be at all ashamed, but that with full courage *now as always Christ will be honored in my body, whether by life or by death (Phil 1:19–20).*

True joy and a total absence of fear ("that I shall not be at all ashamed") always go hand in hand with *parrhēsia* in the most adverse circumstances. Even while under house arrest (Philemon 9) at Rome, Paul writes to Philemon:

Accordingly, though I am bold *enough to command you to do what is required, yet for love's sake I prefer to appeal to you (Phlm 8–9).*

Aware of the "boldness" *(parrhēsia)* that is his, Paul prefers "appeal" *(paraklēsis)* to outright command when writing to a beloved friend. Yet for all that, the appeal is no less frank and outright than a command.

In the Second Letter to the Corinthians Paul sums up the openness of apostolic *parrhēsia* to God and man in the image of the "unveiled face":

Since we have such a hope, we are very bold . . . *when a man turns to the Lord the veil is removed. Now the Lord is the Spirit, and where the Spirit of the Lord is, there is freedom (2 Cor 3:12,16–17).*

Such openness of the apostolic life "has its basis in the gift of the Gospel and its ministry" (Schlier, p. 883). Whoever is in Christ has this freedom of turning both to God and to man. This is why Paul can say to the Corinthians (in the more accurately rendered New English Bible):

I am perfectly frank *with you (2 Cor 7:4);*

and the reason for this frankness is clearly that

We are not, like so many, peddlers of God's word; but as men of sincerity, as commissioned by God, in the sight of God we speak in Christ (2 Cor 2:17).

Any proclaimer of the word finds this liberty of speech, this frankness, not in himself but in the gospel to be

31

proclaimed. The author of 1 Timothy sums up this genuinely Pauline sentiment well:

for those who serve well as deacons gain a good standing for themselves and also great confidence *in the faith which is in Christ Jesus (1 Tim 3:13).*

This then is *parrhēsia* toward God and toward the whole world. It is an "unhampered and joyful word, both in prayer and in dealings with men" (Schlier, p. 883). No obstacles and no "adverse powers" can stop the fearless proclamation of the good news. No outside powers could effectively snuff it out, even though they can severely hinder and cripple its exercise. It is very simply "not the word of men" (1 Thes 2:13). No inadequacy or failure of inner resources can stop it either. It is not a quality of the proclaimer but a free gift of the Lord who is proclaimed. Ultimately, the only thing that could deprive the minister of the word of this gift of *parrhēsia* is the refusal to use it, for whatever seemingly valid reason he or she might devise or invent to explain its non-exercise. "This evangelical freedom of speech shows the message crystal-clear, without admixture; it gives an open character to the relation of the apostle with his fellow-Christians. So *parrhēsia* is a characteristic element of his ministry" (van Unnik, p. 477).

If all this sounds like so much idealistic froth, the following pages hope to show not that it is not—such an effort would be far too pretentious and would prove ultimately fruitless—but to indicate some of the reasons why to many in today's ministry it sounds like that. The previous pages tried to review the data of the New Testament, which—so far as I can determine—have received scant attention in English. What follows can only be the result of personal reflection on such data in the light of present-day experience. This reflection is necessarily conditioned by the writer's own experience, background, prejudice, and all the subjective factors that go to make communication a human venture and not a "technological breakthrough." Such reflection, moreover, is as necessary for the communication of the biblical message as the attentive study of the biblical text itself. For only when the biblical text speaks to me in my own situation today does it become a living word. Inevitably, it remains subject to all the vicissitudes and limitations of life. Of course, any reader can add to these reflections, discount some or even all of them, and modify them in the light of his or her own experience. Reading, after all, is not an exercise in retention but in reflection. We read not so much to remember as to think. Memory is a relatively easy function—machines can do it better; but thought and reflection require effort, and give rise to pain and suffering as well as to light and joy. For the Christian this can be a very fruitful use of the gift of *parrhēsia*; and for the Christian minister such *parrhēsia* is the indispensable mark of *paraklēsis*, the ministry of comfort and consolation in proclaiming the good news of salvation.

Threats to Freedom of Speech

No one can set others free except to the extent that he himself is free. This is of course eminently true of any minister of the word. The proclaimers of salvation in Christ Jesus must not only value their own freedom in order to respect that of others; they must be aware of the grave temptations that beset their own freedom in order to guard others, who are similarly tempted, against them. They must realize, from their own experience at least, that there is no slavery worse than a slavery which is willingly embraced, and no securer bars than those we fashion for our own prisons. The proclaimers of the word know that salvation in Christ means freedom, and that this freedom is an onerous gift which we are only too willing to barter away for facile assurances of salvation other than in the cross of Christ. We are so reluctant to believe that the salvation in Christ is an unearned gift, so prompt to imagine that we can contribute our share to it by submitting to this law, embracing that technique, or following that prescribed procedure.

Saint Paul sums up all our efforts to gain salvation on our own, to find assurance and security in anything but the cross of Christ, under the rubric of "flesh":

For you were called to freedom, brethren; only do not use your freedom as an opportunity for the flesh, but through love be servants of one another (Gal 5:13).

Only those who are genuinely free can give themselves unreservedly to the service of others. Genuine dedication to the service of others must make us keenly sensitive to the allure of the "flesh," the temptation to substitute or to supplement the all-sufficient gift of Christ's salvation with the baubles of personal merit, measurable achievement, and the acclaim of the crowd.

With these brief observations in mind we now turn to our principal concern here. In exercising the ministry of consolation to God's people the minister of the word confronts the constant threat to the *parrhēsia* which is the fearless liberty to

preach the word, be urgent in season and out of season, convince, rebuke, and exhort, be unfailing in patience and in teaching (2 Tim 4:2).

The threats to our freedom of speech today are, understandably enough, different from those of ages past, but they are no less real and every bit as crippling. Perhaps such threats today are less easy to define because they lie hidden under accumulated layers of religious cant, sociopolitical jargon, and trendy psychobabble. Often enough, the most vociferous defenders of our freedom are subtle masters of enslavement, who confuse license with liberty, ideology with faith, and success with salvation.

The following pages, therefore, are a diagnosis, highly personal and—as has already been noted—severely limited by the author's own background, experience, prejudice, and circumscribed—not to say narrow—vision. These are limitations of the human condition shared alike by the writer and his readers. They require recognition rather than apology. The diagnosis here can serve as a sample, may provide a warning, and might perchance be a message of consolation, a *paraklēsis*. Yet, inevitably, such an exercise is bound to be incomplete. The individual reader can alter its particulars, fill out its lacunae, or supplant it altogether with more verifiable experiences. Nevertheless, the diagnosis will have more than served its purpose if it alerts us to some of the dangers that conspire to rob us of our freedom to proclaim the word of salvation.

The Crisis in Preaching

The crisis in the Church today, as often in bygone ages, is a crisis in preaching. The ministers of the word, whatever form their ministry takes and however humble their position might be, experience a severe limitation of their liberty to proclaim the word without fear. It is, to my mind, a far more crippling threat than the dangers besetting the intrepid lions of dogma. As a great Catholic scholar once remarked, when under attack by ecclesiastical authorities: If what I write is false, then the Church is right to silence me; but if what I write is true, then others will come after me to say it, and to say it much better. This is a laudable attitude in a great scholar. But if the ordinary rank and file ministers of the word are robbed, by whatever agency, of their boldness to proclaim the gospel without fear, then an essential and vital function of the Church is affected, the life of faith becomes threatened, hope loses its sense of direction, and love grows cold.

Like any precious gift, the gift of freedom is easy to lose. The freedom to proclaim the word without fear is a precarious possession. Ministers of the word, from the most exalted to the humblest, encounter at every turn those who would rob them of it, hamper its exercise, or relieve them of its responsibility. In order to make this point a bit clearer, it would perhaps be best to divide the threats to the minister's *parrhēsia* into those that arise out of our misunderstanding of the nature of Christian proclamation, and those that affect the person of the minister either by exerting pressures from without or by causing confusion within.

The Christian Proclamation

In describing the threats to a minister's freedom of speech which arise out of a misunderstanding of the nature of Christian proclamation, it would be well to keep in mind that the following points do not concern the qualifications and the preparation of the ministers—to these we shall turn later—but the exercise of their ministry. The anti-intellectualism prevalent in so many quarters today hides under varied guises. But, under whatever guise, such anti-intellectualism is, at best, a pious evasion and, at worst, a ploy to grab power without responsibility, to use a pretended charism as a pretext for evading hard work. Our immediate concern now is with those who, with the proper qualifications and the necessary preparation, undertake the ministry of the word.

One of the first misapprehensions under which so many preachers—particularly those brought up in the "old school"—labor has to do with philosophy. Christian preaching is not the expounding of a philosophic system or the apology for an ideology. The task of the preacher is not to explain and elaborate the premises of a system of thought, be it ever so hallowed and perennial or current and timely. The proclaimer of the word is not called upon to elaborate a coherent treatise on theology within the categories of a philosophy, ancient or modern. The knowledge of philosophy in general or of a given philosophy in particular never was and never can be made the condition for Christian proclamation. Of course, philosophy has an important function to fulfill in preparing the ministers of the word, but it is not what such ministers have to expound from the pulpit or explain in a catechism class. Philosophy can console us for our ignorance, and it should prevent us from being dazzled by what we know; but it is not the subject of Christian proclamation.

When I came to you, brethren, I did not come proclaiming to you the testimony of God in lofty words of wisdom. For I decided to know nothing among you except Jesus Christ and him crucified. And I was with you in weakness and in much fear and trembling; and my speech and my message were not in plausible words of wisdom, but in demonstration of the Spirit and of power, that your faith might not rest in the wisdom of men but in the power of God (1 Cor 2:1–5).

Secondly, and perhaps even more surprisingly to some, Christian preaching is not the teaching of dogma. It is not an exercise in what is called systematic theology. There is, to be sure, an honored and indisputable place for dogma and systematic theology in the Church. But the pulpit is not a lecture stand, nor is a catechism class a course in theology, however inflated the vocabulary of job descriptions be nowadays. Ministers, priests, and catechism teachers are frequently paralyzed into silence or sidetracked into banalities by the fear of their ignorance of the latest insights of biblical scholarship and the most recent theories in dogma. Articles in the popular press—not always a reliable source for theological expertise—peddle the latest in theological fashions. Debates requiring a good deal of mastery of data and subtlety of thought are premasticated into instant pabulum for ready consumption. Speculative ideas and novel theories acquire sudden popularity and just as suddenly vanish into the specialized literature whence they came, there to be challenged, nuanced, modified, or perhaps discarded altogether.

Professional theologians and Scripture scholars are not oracles; none of them enjoys infallibility—all appearances to the contrary notwithstanding. But the general public, under a barrage of inflated clichés ("renowned theologian," "recognized authority," "outstanding scholar," etc.), have little opportunity to assess the worth of theories, follow the course of debates, or weigh their consequences. Scarcely have they had time to assimilate one issue when another novelty replaces the latest fashion; and

As in a theatre, the eyes of men,
After a well-grac'd actor leaves the stage,
Are idly bent on him that enters next,
Thinking his prattle to be tedious.

Amidst this rapidly changing scene, preachers wonder what they can preach on this dogma, what the latest is on that doctrine, and where we stand with regard to that teaching of the Church. Many of those brought up to think that "the Church has always taught" this doctrine and that "the Church has never tolerated" that practice now find themselves wondering about the usefulness of their past training and the adequacy of their present knowledge. They can easily forget that the task of proclaiming the good news is not to parade novelties, nor to purvey popular opinions. The message itself is and remains simple:

For I decided to know nothing among you except Jesus
Christ and him crucified (1 Cor 2:2).

. . . we preach Christ crucified (1 Cor 1:23).

This fact, of course, puts no premium on ignorance of Scripture or incompetence in theology. Anyone proclaiming the word must, to the full measure of his gifts and according to his own abilities, prepare himself and keep abreast of scriptural interpretation and theological reflection. But such necessary accomplishments are conditions for proclaiming the message, not its content.

Needless to say, the above remarks about philosophy and theology are not an apology for ignorance or intellectual sloth. No greater harm can come to the Church than the ignorance of its preachers, teachers, and ministers. The great Saint Francis de Sales wrote:

> *Ignorance in priests is more to be feared than sin . . . knowledge in priests is the eighth sacrament of the ecclesiastical hierarchy; and the Church's greatest misfortunes have come from this, that the ark of knowledge has passed from the Levites into the keeping of others (Hughes, volume III, p. 222).*

Allowance having been made for the age in which these words were written, it remains true that there is no more dangerous kind of minister in the Church today than the one who combines ignorance with zeal. Nothing can wreak more havoc among believers than the minister who mistakes zeal for competence and substitutes enthusiasm for solid learning.

This is not to say that only scholars and professional theologians can minister the word. But it does say that whoever ministers the word, male or female, religious or secular, ordained or lay, must prepare himself to the limit of his ability and continue to do so for the rest of his days. Ministers of the word must surely be aware that the more ignorant our audience, the profounder must our grasp of Scripture and theology be. There is no room here for compromise, and there are no acceptable substitutes. Excess of love and deep compassion cannot make up what is lacking in the competence of a surgeon. They cannot be allowed to blind us to the ignorance of the minister. That there are few malpractice suits brought against ministers in the Church is neither an excuse nor a source of much complacency.

What must be kept in mind here is the nature of the ministry itself. The proclaimers of the word are not there to parade novelties, review on-going debates, or lecture on dogmatic developments. A misconception of what proclaiming the gospel message entails has reduced to virtual silence large numbers of those in the ministry. They are afraid of betraying their ignorance of the latest in theological fashions, unsure of where they stand in the maelstrom of conflicting opinions, ashamed of having been left far behind in the marathon of novelty. One might easily get the impression today that each parish church and every religion class is a miniature Athenian assembly:

Now all the Athenians and the foreigners who lived there spent their time in nothing except telling or hearing something new (Acts 17:21).

Finally, the proclamation of the Christian message must not be confounded with the métier of the psychologist or the psychiatrist, however valuable and necessary these may be in today's world. Neither a degree in theology nor ordination to the ministry confers competence in either psychology or psychiatry. The minister of the word must not confuse the call to repentance and the proclamation of freedom in Christ and the forgiveness of sins with the "business of the psychotherapist" (Bultmann, p. 239). The current jargon of mental health cannot be substituted for "Peace I leave with you; my peace I give to you. ... Let not your hearts be troubled, neither let them be afraid" (Jn 14:27). It is so easy to clothe the Christian message with the jargon of today's psychotherapy, so easy to confuse the peace of Christ with "mental health." Whatever may be said for the rapprochement of religion with today's therapeutic sciences—and a great deal can indeed be said for such rapprochement—the minister of the word cannot forget that the word proclaimed is a call to repentance, a challenge to commitment, and a summons to service in love. Inevitably, it is a word that disturbs our facile security, uproots our self-confidence, and calls for unconditional faith in a God who is the sole source of our salvation. The proclamation of the word is a call to "stand firm in your faith" (2 Cor 1:24), not to "nullify the grace of God" (Gal 2:21), and not to yield to the temptation to remove "the stumbling block of the cross" (Gal 5:11). It is a constant reminder that

> whoever would save his life will lose it, and whoever loses his life for my sake will find it (Mt 16:25; cf. 10:39).

Only thus can the ministry of the word become a ministry of consolation, a *paraklēsis*. The analyst cannot replace the confessor; nor can the confessor pretend to be an analyst, however fashionable such "Freudulant" ministry might be today.

Of course, such a list of common misapprehensions can be prolonged. It will have served its purpose adequately, however, if it alerted the ministers of the word to the common misconceptions that beset the object of their ministry. Fads and fashions must not be allowed to distract us from the basically simple message of salvation in Jesus Christ. In this day and age it is difficult and demanding enough to prepare for such a ministry without confusing its object with the sum of human knowledge. Competence, not omniscience, is what is required of the minister. But the ministry of the word is not the occasion to display our intellectual wares and academic achievements. The word to be proclaimed is not man's word but God's. If it requires study and learning on the part of the ministers—as it indeed does—that study and learning is necessary in order to keep them ever jealous of the integrity of the message, careful to distinguish personal opinion from divine revelation (see 1 Cor 7:12), and slow to confuse their own preferences with the will of God in Jesus Christ.

"The War Within"

A misunderstanding of the object of our proclamation, of what it is we must preach and teach and exhort, can rob us of our freedom of speech as surely as any tyrannous force exerted on us from outside. Such external forces can be crippling enough. They are today all the more menacing because they come masquerading as angels of light. The tyranny of mad emperors or of totalitarian regimes was, by comparison, easier to bear. Indeed, it bred illustrious witnessees to the faith in every age, as it begets in our own day fearless proclaimers of the word, whose names and number are known only to God.

But be the war within, the brand we wield
Unseen, the heroic breast not outward-steeled,
Earth hears no hurtle then from fiercest fray.

It is to this "war within" that we now must turn. We consider here the threat to our liberty that either comes from outside us or is at work within us. The outside threats may be sorted, for convenience, into those that come from institutions and those posed by individuals, although it is not always easy in actual experience to distinguish one from another. Institutions after all are not disembodied entities. They are made up of individuals who, as often as not, enunciate policies, interpret aims, and execute plans. Our encounter with such individuals, our views of and our judgments on them are what we mean usually when we express our reaction to this or that church, government, convent, monastery, or school. This is an important point to keep in mind because, if we belong to any institution whatever, then we must realize that its administrators and spokesmen are individuals chosen from among us. Nations, it is said, have the governments they deserve. Is this any less true of churches, congregations, monasteries, or convents? Experience ought to have taught us to be a bit skeptical about our facile censoriousness of the institutions to which we belong. Critics often imply, and just as often express, the conviction that they could and would do a better job running this department or that church. Alas, all too often, given such a chance, they turn out worse than their predecessors at the task, those who were the objects of their most intemperate criticisms. This is not simply because, as is often said, "Authority corrupts." The tragedy lies much deeper:

Under three things the earth trembles;
under four it cannot bear up:
a slave when he becomes king . . .
and a maid when she succeeds her mistress (Prov 30:21–23; cf. 19:10).

Slaves make tyrannous masters.

In any consideration of the threats to our liberty that arise out of institutions, this has to be kept in mind. Once in a position to do so, we are, all of us, prompt to make our pet notions the will of the Almighty, to regard our own views as the universal norm for reasonable action, and our understanding as the infallible guide to the truth. Those who in every generation give the lie to this assertion are precisely the rare individuals who, having known true freedom even in the lowliest of positions, set others free when they assume the reigns of power and exercise authority. No succession of bitter experiences can be allowed to make us forget those individuals who, in places of authority, set others free precisely because they assumed power in order "to serve and not to be served."

True authority in the Church is service:

If any one would be first, he must be last of all and servant of all (Mk 9:35).

This service is always in direct ratio to the minister's freedom in Christ Jesus:

For you were called to freedom . . . through love be servants of one another (Gal 5:13).

For, as has already been remarked above, to set others free one has to be free oneself. To proclaim redemption to others one has to know what it is to be redeemed and to understand what redemption really means.

A little lucidity about ourselves and about those who "make the rules" should go a long way toward safeguarding our own freedom. Preparation for ministry in the Church need not always be a study in slavery:

> *But just as we have been approved by God to be entrusted with the gospel, so we speak, not to please men, but to please God who tests our hearts (1 Thes 2:4).*

There is every good reason why any minister of the word must first meet certain requirements and achieve specific goals. These requirements and goals are, or at least should be, designed simply to make sure that the minister can be "entrusted with the gospel." They are not devised in order "to please men," to conform to the pet prejudices of those in charge, to bolster up their egos, or to advance their hierarchical ambitions. The requirements and the goals are themselves basically within the reach of any "average intelligence" willing to exert itself and to expend the needed energy. But, ultimately, it is God "who tests our hearts." The proclamation of the gospel is not the exclusive domain of mandarins, nor the privileged preserve of academicians. There is, on the other hand, no reason why the ministry should be the refuge of the intellectually bankrupt or the demonstrable failures in other walks of life.

Nevertheless, a double danger besets anyone intent upon preparing for the ministry of the word today. One danger is from the "accrediting institutions," which frequently give the impression that the Way is but a lane off Wall Street. It is so easy to succumb, even in the most sacred institutions, to the spirit of competition and the lure of success. It is easier still to lose sight of the goal: to prepare myself to the best of my ability and, using the gifts that are mine from God, to serve the word in the Church. This requires a lucidity about myself, my gifts, my abilities, and my limitations. It requires an equal lucidity about institutions and a measure of skepticism about the bloated rhetoric employed by those who run them. But above all it requires great fortitude of soul to accept myself on my own rung of the ladder and not to be misled into a spirit of competition that blinds me to the nature of my calling "to serve and not to reign" and misguides my steps into the labyrinth of techniques and gimmicks and the current fashions. Such a competitive spirit deludes me into accepting the achievements of others as my goals, and misleads me into believing that their success—and, consequently, mine too—is contingent upon clever methods and novel techniques. It makes me lose sight of the fact that the word I proclaim is "not the word of man" but of God (1 Thes 2:13).

The other danger besetting our liberty to proclaim the word comes from those to whom we proclaim it. Accustomed to the evanescent dazzle of star performers in the media and subjected to a barrage of the inflated adjectives that herald their performances, Christian believers often transfer the former to expectations from, and the latter to standards for, those who minister the word to them. Little experience is needed to teach us the insidious attraction of this to any minister of the word. To succumb to it is to yield up our precious liberty to proclaim that word without fear. Such flattering expectations and the delusive adjectives of my inflated excellence can give me the short-lived thrill of imagined achievement and shore up my sagging self-confidence; but they inevitably rob me of my liberty to speak the word of the cross to a world too busy chanting the alleluias of ersatz resurrections. There are few slaveries more cruel than the expectations of others.

The word of the cross, however, saps our smugness, overthrows our cherished ideas and undermines our security. Its proclamation does not always leave undisturbed our orderly plans and our well-plotted charts for the future. Should the exercise of *parrhēsia* disrupt the placid flow of the congregation's established routine, the custodians of order will hasten to its defense. The "voice of authority" will sound its clarion call to order. Should this go unheeded, the custodians of order will assure you that, of course, what you say is not new, that the church "has always taught this," and that you evidently have abundant gifts for joining them in spreading the message. Indeed, just to make things easier for you, they are willing to erect a building, purchase equipment, provide assistants, and promote you to a rank worthy of your apostolate. In a word, they will co-opt you. How many fearless proclaimers of the word have yielded their freedom of speech for some elevated position in a parish or diocese, for a superior's post or a bishopric, or for some dignity in the Church at large!

If, by some miracle—not as rare in the annals of the Church as we might despondently imagine—all these cajolements fail to win you over, then, ironically enough, you are reminded of the great virtue of humility, and measures are taken to secure your possession of it. The disciplining authorities easily forget that it takes genuine humility to have withstood the past successive attempts on the gift of *parrhēsia*. If I know I have nothing that I did not receive (1 Cor 4:7), if I really believe that "a servant is not greater than his master" (Jn 13:16), then the reminder of humility is just that, a reminder; and the devised humilitations ought to cause no surprise even though they bring added suffering.

A disciple is not above his master, nor a servant above his master; it is enough for the disciple to be like his teacher, and the servant like his master (Mt 10:24–25).

The suffering is all the more acute because it comes from those whom we respect in the Lord:

But we beseech you, brethren, to respect those who labor among you and are over you in the Lord and admonish you, and to esteem them very highly in love because of their work (1 Thes 5:12–13).

It is all the harder to bear such suffering because it cuts me off from those to whom I am bound with ties of love and reverence. But, inevitably, to be free is a terribly solitary stance. The solitude is further accentuated by the knowledge of my own limitations and by my implicit trust in the good will of those over me. It is a stunted infantilism that would make me believe that I have exclusive grasp of absolute truth, or imagine that all those who oppose me are selfish fools misguided by blind ambition.

The balance, evidently, is difficult to maintain, and the very effort to maintain it gives edge to the temptation to relinquish my freedom to proclaim the word in exchange for the momentary relief of suffering or for the remedy to the solitude of freedom. But a steadying force in the midst of all this is the realization that I do not enjoy my liberty to proclaim the word because of any natural talents I possess, any intellectual accomplishments I call my own, or any elevated position I occupy within the Christian community. A minister of the word is someone who is called, who has a mission:

> *And how can men preach unless they are sent? (Rom 10:15).*

In his first sermon Karl Barth reminded his Safenwil congregation, "I am not speaking of God because I am a pastor; I am a pastor because I *must* speak to you of God." These words of the great theologian are but a faithful echo of Saint Paul's reminder to the Corinthians:

> *For if I preach the gospel, that gives me no ground for boasting. For necessity is laid upon me. Woe to me if I do not preach the gospel! (1 Cor 9:16).*

These words in turn express the awesome burden of the office of prophecy in the Church in every age:

> *If I say, "I will not mention him,*
> *or speak any more in his name,"*
> *there is in my heart as it were a burning fire*
> *shut up in my bones,*
> *and I am weary with holding it in,*
> *and I cannot" (Jer 20:9).*

This compulsion to speak is at the very source of the proclaimer's freedom to proclaim the word without fear or hindrance. It is what gave the Old Testament prophets their sense of mission and the consequent courage to speak the unpalatable truth to their contemporaries. It is what made Paul both bold enough to oppose Peter to his face (Gal 2:11) and sure enough of himself to write the Corinthians

out of much affliction and anguish of heart and many tears, not to cause you pain but to let you know the abundant love that I have for you (2 Cor 2:4).

Only those who truly love can speak the painful truth to the object of their love. Neither eminence of position nor lowliness of state can allow us to forget this. Without this love the liberty of speech is almost always either overbearing despotism in the superior or carping insolence in the subject.

The ministry of the word is, and must always be, a service of love: love of the word itself, and love of those to whom and for whose sake it is proclaimed. Only thus can it be a ministry of consolation exercised with sovereign freedom. Only thus can that freedom be safeguarded against the coercions from above and the erosions from below. It is only when "the love of Christ controls us" that we can "regard no one from a human point of view" (2 Cor 5:14,16); and therein lies the genuine Christian freedom of speech.

"My Equal, My Companion, My Familiar Friend"

We have thus far considered the dangers to our freedom of speech in proclaiming the word that arise out of two sources: from our own misunderstanding of the nature of the word and from what might be called—for lack of a better term—the "institution." But, real though such dangers are, they do not compare with the danger we pose to one another in the exercise of our ministry.

A brief reflection on our experience should convince us that the greater danger to our liberty of speech comes from the ordinary people with whom we work and to whom we minister. Few, very few of us are summoned "before the synagogues and the rulers and the authorities" (Luke 12:11). If we have any anxiety about "what we are to say," if we are paralyzed into silence, the cause to seek for most of us is nothing so exalted as "governors and kings"—whether ecclesiastical or civil. Today's media speak as though a new Inquisition is afoot; some ministers of the word are tempted to act as though it were. There is, paradoxically enough, a sense of self-importance to be derived from imagining one's liberty of speech constantly imperiled by some scarlet eminence slipping in "to spy on our freedom which we have in Christ Jesus, that they might bring us into bondage" (Gal 2:4). But, ecclesiastical gossip and the popular media notwithstanding, the real danger to our freedom of speech in ministering the word comes from much humbler quarters. It comes from those who, in the words of the psalmist, are "my equal, my companion, my familiar friend" with whom we hold "sweet converse together" and walk in fellowship "within God's house" (Ps 55:13–14). It comes from those with whom our daily life is spent: colleagues and parishioners and students.

The threats to our liberty here are those we pose to one another in everyday life. We are all—understandably enough—anxious to know that we do not labor "in vain" (1 Thes 3:5). Equally understandable is the encouragement we offer and receive from one another. But this encouragement, whether in words of congratulations or in marks of approval, is so often tinged with just a hint of superior knowledge on the part of the one offering it. An unexpressed "of course, there is some room for improvement" lurks in the background. It is as though the offer of support and encouragement is conditional upon your acceptance of the advice offered. There is just a hint that the one congratulating you possesses the secret of making your good a little better.

To anyone reluctant to discriminate between "worldly success" and fruitful ministry, to anyone foolish enough to imagine a state where there is no room for improvement, a state attainable here on earth, such temptation is irresistible. If I labor "to please men" or to "seek glory from men" (1 Thes 2:4,6) then the price I have to pay is my liberty to proclaim the word. In the ministry of the word it is God, and God alone, who "gives the growth" (1 Cor 3:7). We can, of course, be of inestimable help in encouraging one another in the difficult, and often thankless, task of proclaiming the gospel; but we must be ever on our guard lest we use such encouragement to subject one another to our own way of thinking, our own pet ideas, or our own preferred modes of approach. Genuine, liberating praise always comes from those who deeply rejoice, not in seeing their own camp augmented by new followers, but in seeing the word itself advance and prosper. It takes profound humility to realize, no matter how loud the acclaim and how enthusiastic the applause, that

God chose what is low and despised in the world, even things that are not, so that no human being might boast in the presence of God. ... What then is Apollos? What is

Paul? Servants through whom you believed, as the Lord assigned to each. I planted, Apollos watered, but God gave the growth. So neither he who plants nor he who waters is anything, but only God who gives the growth (1 Cor 1:28–29; 3:5–7).

We are in fact the "low and despised in the world." In order to see how this is indeed so, one has only to preach what the world—whether inside the Church or outside it—refuses to hear. We have only to reject the world's standards of success, refuse to submit to its spirit of competition, or spurn its proffered accolades to learn the price we really have to pay for our freedom in Christ. We have only to espouse the unpopular or refuse to champion the fashionable to find out how few there are who are willing to offer unfeigned praise or lend disinterested support. But perhaps the almost infallible test today would be to take a stand against some crusade currently in vogue, to dare to raise a question conveniently side-stepped by the popular orthodoxy of the day, or to suggest that perhaps the view of legitimate authority merits consideration. It is then that we discover how unliberal the very champions of "liberalism" can be. Bertrand Russell once wrote: "The essence of the Liberal outlook lies not in what opinions are held but in how they are held; instead of being held dogmatically, they are held tentatively." To find out how truly "dogmatic" the current liberalism can be, one has only to challenge any of its conclusions, question one of its premises, or merely suggest that tradition and the past have some claim on our attention.

The subtlest threats to our Christian freedom, however, are perhaps those that come from people to whom we minister the word. Theology—more than any of the comtemporary fields of pandemic omniscience such as psychology, politics or the weather—is everybody's competence, or so it seems. The tribe of quondam "altar boys" knows no decrease even in these days when religious sentiment is supposedly on the wane. Many of the Christians you address, however earnestly they might protest their ignorance and incompetence, imagine themselves theologians. If what you say agrees with what they believe, they thank you for "sharing" with them. If it does not, they protest that this is not what "the good sisters" taught them. Of course, every minister of the word ought to realize that neither response can be summarily dismissed in the name of freedom to proclaim the word. The sense of the believers and the consensus of the faithful are not only necessary in the Church but have their effectiveness guaranteed by the Holy Spirit. Else, how could the Christian community judge:

If any one is preaching to you a gospel contrary to that which you received, let him be accursed (Gal 1:9)?

It is the realization of this fact that renders the threats posed by those to whom we proclaim the word so subtle and so hard to define.

Perhaps a few instances of such threats might sufficiently illustrate, if not successfully demonstrate, the reality of the danger they pose. There is, particularly today, a widespread belief that we all have a right to the very best in teachers, preachers, and ministers. On the other hand, there is a corresponding reluctance to accept the simple fact that, even in the most democratic of societies, the best is by definition a very limited category. It is this reluctance that breeds the myths of excellence which we apply so readily to those who proclaim the word to us in any capacity. The humblest of gatherings is assured that the one addressing them is a "world authority," a "renowned scholar," or some author whose works are "too numerous to mention." Of course, no one in the assembly stands up to inquire what any of these esteemed and, perhaps, highly desirable qualifications have to do with the proclamation of the word.

> *Where is the wise man? Where is the scribe? Where is the debater of this age? . . . When I came to you, brethren, I did not come proclaiming to you the [mystery] of God in lofty words of wisdom (1 Cor 1:20; 2:1).*

The most elementary of classes—to take another, but closely allied instance—is impatient with the humble rudiments of instruction in the faith. There is little enthusiasm to discuss anything but the most abtruse and nebulous questions of religion. One might well wonder how willing anybody is in today's Church to be fed "with milk, not solid food," or to be reminded that he is "not ready" for the latter (1 Cor 3:2). It is so very easy to forget our need for "milk" before we are ready for "solid food." Indeed, there is almost an implicit disdain of any beginner's fare in religious matters. Primers do not make best sellers nowadays. It seems beneath our intellectual dignity to learn the rudiments of the faith that the Church professed in past centuries; we are far too intent upon fashioning a faith for the future. History and tradition are not the "in" subjects today.

Subjected to the pressures of something akin to the mercantile laws of demand and supply, the minister of the word often either tacitly accepts the unearned and untrue adjectives to play a role, or, unable to acquiesce in the fallacious accolades, lapses into silence. There is an unwillingness to face any crowd with the frank admission of my ignorance of, say, world religions, the psychology of faith, or the morality of nuclear war. It is so easy under such pressure to forget that

I decided to know nothing among you except Jesus Christ and him crucified (1 Cor 2:1–2).

Admittedly, this is a one-sided view, almost a caricature of the situation. But anyone ministering the word in today's Church must have felt the insidious attraction of the current fashions: the trendy titles for sermons, the high-sounding names for courses of religious instruction, the prevalence of the stillborn jargon of the social sciences, the inflated value of "terminal" degrees for the humblest ministry. The price a minister pays for this is ultimately exacted from his freedom to proclaim the word. The eagerness to please, to be modern, to cater to the ceaseless craving for novelty—all these can, and do, rob me of carrying out a basically simple—though far from easy—task of proclaiming the gospel.

For we are not, like so many, peddlers of God's word; but as men of sincerity, as commissioned by God, in the sight of God, we speak in Christ (2 Cor 2:17).

It takes very little experience in the ministry today to realize how necessary and needed is the proclamation of the gospel in its most fundamental form, what the author of Hebrews calls the "first principles of God's word"

(5:12). This is a most demanding task, far more demanding than the imposing debates on the outer frontiers of dogma. Such a task requires, inevitably, a solid grasp of the gospel message, its meaning and its implications. Indeed, the less sophisticated the people to whom I am called to proclaim the message, the surer must my grasp of it be. This is no easy job. Anyone acquainted, even at second hand, with the preparation for ministry must know how much, not genius, but hard and dedicated work it requires. In this enterprise, genius is hard work. To pretend otherwise, to plead one's own intellectual insufficiency or the unsophisticated requirements of a community, is an evasion of the stringent demands of a task that is never ending, the task of maintaining a secure grasp on "the first principles of God's word." It requires hard and dedicated labor throughout one's life in the ministry.

Such work and dedication will inevitably set the ministers of the word in a special category. They are, willy-nilly, "leaders, those who spoke to you the word of God" (Heb 13:7). This might offend the currently popular "democratic" ideals that some entertain for the Church. But what distinguishes the Church is not that it has no hierarchy but that precisely anyone in its hierarchy is "last of all and servant of all" (Mk 9:35). The hard and continued labor involved in ministering the word is but fidelity to a calling, not a means of advancement. It is an amusing sight in today's Church to see how those most jealous of the democratic ideals for the Church are readiest to forget the only true evangelical basis of any "democracy" in the Church:

Whoever would be first among you must be slave of all (Mk 10:44).

But, however one may wish to describe the phenomenon, in the Church there are, as there were and always shall be, the teachers and the taught, those who are "over you in the Lord and admonish you" (1 Thes 5:12) and those who are under them and admonished by them, those who minister and those to whom they minister. Since not all are "apostles . . . prophets . . . teachers" (1 Cor 12:29), there is a general scramble—as in Corinth of old—for the "preferred positions." It is so very easy for ministers in the Church to forget that

Whoever would be great among you must be your servant, and whoever would be first among you must be your slave (Mt 20:26–27).

Ministers who forget this simple fact of the Christian ministry readily assume an almost apologetic attitude toward its exercise. They forget that the ministry is not a right but a calling, not a privilege but a burden. They have not been called because of any natural advantage or acquired accomplishment of their own. Their calling is certainly not to "lord it over" or "to exercise authority over" the Christian community (cf. Mt. 20:25). If they must have a title to greatness, then it can be no other than their title to humble service of all. If they are first in anything it is in being "slaves" to the people they serve:

You know that the rulers of the Gentiles lord it over them, and their great men exercise authority over them. It shall not be so among you; but whoever would be great among you must be your servant, and whoever would be first among you must be your slave (Mt 20:25–27).

It is in this specifically non-Christian, Gentile, mentality of quest for first positions and the machinations of power that still another threat lurks for them who exercise the ministry of the word. For, within such a framework of "power politics," the next best thing to occupying a position of power is to befriend those who wield it. The minister of the word can fall a ready prey to today's pervasive easy familiarity and the subtle enticements of friendship. A short while before he died, Dietrich Bonhoeffer wrote, "Unless we have the courage to fight for a revival of wholesome reserve between man and man, we shall perish in an anarchy of human values. The impudent contempt for such reserve is the mark of the rabble . . . ." This is never easy to say and always difficult to keep in mind. What gave Bonhoeffer the courage to say it was not his social status, but his experience of living in a time when "Hope had grown grey hairs,/Hope had mourning on,/Trenched with tears, carved with cares . . . ."

Of course, we all want to be loved. The genuine item is so precious a gift that all of us are ready to settle even for the nearest imitation. But such easy offers of love and friendship exact a dear price from our freedom to speak without hindrance. It takes great fortitude of spirit to pronounce an adroit No! to today's facile blandishments of friendship. It takes a wary vigilance to eschew the religious and saccharine cant propagated by the "peddlers of God's word."

The message of salvation we proclaim brings the good news of "deliverance to the captives." It ill becomes a minister of such a message to make of the very act of its proclamation an instrument of subjugation, however willing the victims. The word proclaimed is not a prelude to social pleasantries, but a challenge to total surrender to the way of the cross. "For a good purpose," wrote Saint

Paul, "it is always good to be made much of" (Gal 4:18). Yet those very Galatians who had once received him "as an angel of God, as Christ Jesus" (4:14), who were willing to pluck out their eyes and give them to him (4:15), turned against him:

Have I then become your enemy by telling you the truth? (Gal 4:16).

It would have been—it always is—so easy to compromise, attenuate the message in exchange for their good will and their friendship. But Paul's task, like the task of all those who follow him, was not to collect fans, assemble factions, or gather cliques. It was, and always will be, to address a message that sets its true hearers free, free to be themselves, and free to be wholly for others. The word addressed to them is a word of "consolation," not because it suffuses them with pious feelings and distracts them from their present ills, but because it gives them the courage and the patience to pay the high price of being truly themselves in being wholly for others.

Only by being wholly for others, whoever these might be and wherever they happen to be, can the ministers of the word be genuinely

servants of Christ and stewards of the mysteries of God (1 Cor 4:1).

This is ultimately what gave Paul—and what gives every minister—the courage to say:

But with me it is a very small thing that I should be judged by you or by any human court. I do not even judge myself. . . . It is the Lord who judges me (1 Cor 4:3).

Here, finally, is the heart of the problem: our inveterate tendency to play the judge on ourselves. Even those of us most reluctant to judge others are most ready to exercise such judgment, without mercy or pity, on themselves: the soundness of their teaching, the efficacy of their methods, the "purity" of their intentions, the success of their endeavors. This deep-rooted tendency to judge my self, my actions, my success and failure, is what makes me easy prey to the lure of the fashionable in doctrine, the attraction of the popular in methods, and the insatiable quest for "support and affirmation" from every quarter, like

children, tossed to and fro and carried about with every wind of doctrine, by the cunning of men, by their craftiness in deceitful wiles (Eph 4:14).

But the inner courtroom is a strangely empty place when the demon of doubt is abroad. There is today a vacuum of authority in the Church. Perhaps it is about to be, or maybe already being, filled. History should reassure us that it will be filled—for better or worse. Meanwhile, the vacuum is there resounding to echoes of the would-be claimants to authority. Witnesses—at several removes—to all these claims and counterclaims, many of today's ministers wonder about the relevance, if not the orthodoxy, of what they preach and teach. Others, anxious to be abreast of the latest developments, find themselves outmoded before they have had time to grasp fully whatever—only yesterday—occupied the popular press and captured the public fancy. An issue is one day a deadly dogma and the next a dead letter. This, of course, only compounds the doubt for the ministers of the word, while ecclesiastical authority, like a character in Dickens, responds to any challenge to her authority by exaggerating her original statement. All this might be viewed as quite healthy, or even amusing, were it not for the fact that most Christians have been brought up to link right teaching with salvation and all error with eternal damnation. They know, as do their ministers, that what you believe does make a difference.

In every exercise of judgment upon one's own ministry the spectre of failure looms forbidding. What adds terror to its threatening visage is the fact that there are today so many and such varied claims for the nature of the ministry, its scope and its purpose. It is hard to measure success in such an ill-defined task. The multiplicity of views on the ministry today, useful and necessary though they be for an enhanced understanding of its meaning, unwittingly give the impression of being criteria for success. Rare is the minister who can withstand the onslaught of charts and statistics demonstrating the efficacy of this approach or the proven results of that method. Rarer still perhaps is the minister who can say with Paul:

> *Such is the confidence that we have through Christ toward God. Not that we are sufficient of ourselves to claim anything as coming from us; our sufficiency is from God, who has qualified us to be ministers of a new covenant. . . . Therefore, having this ministry by the mercy of God, we do not lose heart (2 Cor 3:4–6; 4:1).*

This is the source of Paul's *parrhēsia* and the source whence every minister of the word derives the courage to speak openly and freely and without fear. The source of this *parrhēsia* is inexhaustible because it depends not on the vagaries of men, on their ever-changing tastes, or on their fluctuating standards. It arises out of a clear vision of the work of the ministry as God's work. It is by "the mercy of God," not by the approbation and approval of men, that we have this ministry. God alone is the judge of its efficacy. He alone "gives the growth."

Such lucidity about the ministry can come only from faith. In the midst of the solitude that is inevitably ours in the exercise of the ministry, a solitude accentuated by the uncertainty and the confusion around us, such a faith is the only sure safeguard of our freedom of speech in proclaiming the gospel. The body of Christ, after all, is not a social club or a political gathering. It is not the exclusive preserve of the intellectual elite or the bastion of mitered authority. It surely is not a debating society for the clever and wise "debater of this age" (1 Cor 1:19–20), nor an arena for the agile picadors of dogma.

It takes faith to believe that God does actually choose "what is foolish in the world ... what is weak in the world ... what is low and despised in the world ... so that no human being might boast in the presence of God" (1 Cor 1:27–29). No minister of the word is exempted from these humbling categories by reason of native talents, academic degrees, scholarly distinctions, or ecclesiastical dignity. If claim to equality there be in the Church it is this:

> So let no one boast of men. For all things are yours ... and you are Christ's; and Christ's is God's (1 Cor 3:21–23).

Conclusion

"We have this treasure in earthen vessels," fragile,

forever threatened, requiring constant vigilance. The preceding pages tried to call attention to some of the dangers which menace the precious possession of our Christian freedom under only one of its aspects: in the proclamation of the word of salvation, *paraklēsis*, the "ministry of consolation."

The Christian freedom of speech, *parrhēsia*, possesses characteristics of meaning that distinguish it from its background even while it maintains its etymological attachments to the Gentile soil whence it came. One can speak, justifiably I believe, of a specifically Christian *parrhēsia* which, even when it needs its Greek background and origin for the proper grasp of its meaning, is a distinctly religious term that became part of the Christian stock vocabulary very early in the first century.

What started out as a term closely allied to the political life of the free citizen in the Athenian democracy of the fifth century B.C. ended up as a philosophical term describing aspects, both good and bad, of social intercourse. By the first century A.D., *parrhēsia*'s meaning had altered quite significantly from the political to the ethical and social.

True knowledge begins with the definition of terms; and it was that great definer of terms, Aristotle, who, in the fourth century B.C., directed the course of *parrhēsia* into new channels. He still defined the term as a virtue of the freeborn citizen but, significantly, associated it with the magnanimous person, "the great-souled man" who must be "open both in love and in hate . . . and care more for the truth than for what people will think . . . is outspoken and frank" (*Nicomachean Ethics* IV, 3). So from a political concept *parrhēsia* was on its way to becoming a moral virtue.

There are, to be sure, reasons for this change. One of them was the decline of democratic ideals. Changes in the political climate made the exercise of *parrhēsia*, the freedom of the citizen to "say anything," quite difficult and sometimes ill-advised. Aristotle himself, shortly after the death of his pupil, Alexander the Great, came to know the "bitter bread of banishment." This is, of course, not the whole explanation. Yet the fact remains that, once *parrhēsia* entered the field of the moral virtues, it took two different courses. It became a term either of the private or of the public moral life of the individual.

In the private sphere, *parrhēsia* became the virtue that marks the relationship between two friends, "belonging to friendship only." Its opposite, understandably enough, became "flattery," "counterfeit frankness," as Plutarch called it. As a matter of fact, Plutarch, the popular—in the best sense of the word—philosopher of the first century (A.D. 45-120, the years within which the New Testament books were written), wrote an essay on "How To Tell a Flatterer from a Friend." It can fairly be described as an essay on the uses and abuses of *parrhēsia* in human relationships. Its first part deals with "certain fatal faults attending upon frankness," and hence with flattery and its ways; while the second part is a "disquisition on frank speech (*parrhēsia*)," which Plutarch himself calls "the language of friendship especially."

In the public sphere, on the other hand, *parrhēsia* became the distinguishing mark of the Cynic philosopher. The name "Cynic," which comes from the Greek word for "dog," goes back to the fourth century B.C. philosopher, Diogenes of Sinope, "the snapping dog who thought it his vocation to revise all prevailing values." The Cynics, who valued "freedom and frankness" among the highest virtues, maintained that the morally free person possesses *parrhēsia*. Here, clearly, *parrhēsia* has become a manifestation of the inner moral disposition of the individual. If he is "morally free," if he has what Aristotle called "greatness of soul," then *parrhēsia* characterizes his morally upright dealings with others. Should the individual be subject to the baser passions, then his *parrhēsia* can be no more than outright insolence.

In his *Lives of Eminent Philosophers,* Diogenes Laertius relates that, when asked what the most beautiful thing in the world is, Diogenes of Sinope replied, "Freedom of speech." Evidently, there were those who disagreed. Whether *parrhēsia* is beautiful freedom or intolerable insolence depends as much on the reaction of the hearer as on the inner disposition of the speaker.

However, the remarkable thing in the use of the term and its development is the absence of these connotations from the New Testament usage of *parrhēsia*. Plutarch's contemporary use of the term as a concomitant of friendship and the Cynics' esteem of it as a moral virtue (or vice) were both clearly current knowledge in the century of the New Testament. Indeed, one of the most successful achievements of the Cynics was the literary form of "diatribe," which is so much in evidence in the epistles of Paul. Yet, neither Paul nor any of the other authors of the New Testament reflects any of the Plutarchian or Cynic connotations of *parrhēsia*. The term seems to have taken a hithertho untrodden path when it entered the field of New Testament writings.

Why was this so? Part of the explanation has to do with the use of the term Septuagint, as has already been indicated above. But, when we consider *parrhēsia* as the freedom of speech in proclaiming the Christian message, the rest of the explanation is not far to seek. Though they did not set out expressly to explain the reasons behind the Christian understanding of *parrhēsia*, the above pages should and—I earnestly hope—did provide some such reasons. It remains for me to draw them out by way of conclusion.

The ministers of the word exercise their freedom of speech in function of their faith in Christ Jesus. Their *paraklēsis*, their ministry of consolation, is but a response to the gift they acknowledge to be theirs by the mercy of God revealed in Christ. Their awareness of God as both the ultimate source of their sufficiency and the sole judge of their labor renders them truly fearless in carrying out their ministry of the word.

As ministers, they are servants of Christ, who set the norm and pattern for their ministry by his death on the cross. If their ministry gives them any claim at all, it is the claim to be "last of all and servants of all." They know that their commissioning by God is his choice of the foolish, the weak, the low and the despised of this world "so that no human being might boast in the presence of God."

It is this realization of the significance of their calling that gives the ministers of the word the needed clarity of vision to regard no one "from a human point of view." They know that a necessity is laid upon them to speak the word fearlessly, in season and out of season. They know too that the word they proclaim is not the word of man but the word of God. It is God alone who assures its growth. It is, ultimately, God's word which

shall not return to me empty,
but it shall accomplish that which I purpose,
and prosper in the thing for which I sent it (Is 55:11).

Therefore, in the very exercise of their ministry of the word lies the unshakable conviction that their freedom to speak openly and without fear, their *parrhēsia*, is but their way of being servants of one another through love.

Bibliography

The page references in the body of the text are to the following works:

Rudolf Bultmann, "Preaching: Genuine and Secularized," in *Religion and Culture. Essays in Honor of Paul Tillich,* edited by Walter Leibrecht (New York: Harper and Bros., 1959), pp. 236–242.

Philip Hughes, *A History of the Church,* Volume 3 (London: Sheed & Ward, 1947).

A. Momigliano, "The Social Structure of the Ancient City," in S. C. Humphreys, *Anthropology and the Greeks* (London: Routledge and Kegan Paul, 1978), pp. 177–193.

Heinrich Schlier, *"parrhēsia,"* in Gerhard Kittel, ed., *Theological Dictionary of the New Testament,* Volume V (Grand Rapids: Wm. B. Eerdmans, 1967), pp. 871–886.

Otto Schmitz and Gustav Stählin, *"parakaleō, paraklēsis,"* in Gerhard Kittel, ed., *Theological Dictionary of the New Testament,* Volume V, pp. 773–799.

Joseph Thomas, "Athènes ou Corinthe. Le métier de prédicateur," *Christus* 15 (57, 1968) 61–72.

W. C. van Unnik, "The Christian's Freedom of Speech in the New Testament," *Bulletin of the John Rylands Library* 44 (1962) 466–488.